Using Steam
to Make Electricity

We can make electricity.

We can make electricity
with water.

We can make electricity
with wind.

We can make electricity
with the sun.

5

Look at this.

We can make electricity

with this too.

Woosh!

The water goes up.

The water goes up

and up and up.

Can you see the **steam**?

The steam is hot.

The steam will go

on the **wheel.**

The steam will make the wheel

go round and round.

This will make electricity.

The electricity is made here.

Glossary

 steam

 wheel